FOCUS
ON THE FINISH LINE

Hurdles Female Athletes Face in the Race of Life

by Dr. Elliot Johnson

FOCUS
ON THE FINISH LINE

Hurdles Female Athletes Face in the Race of Life

CONTENTS

IDENTITY: Who Are You?

6 • #1 COMPETING ON THE ENEMY'S
"HOME COURT"
9 • #2 WHEN YOUR PRACTICE DOESN'T MATCH
YOUR POSITION
14 • #3 A HEALTHY SELF-IMAGE
16 * #4 ROLE MODELS—IT TAKES ONE TO BECOME ONE

ATTITUDE: What do you think?

18 • #5 LISTENING TO THE RIGHT VOICES
20 • #6 TEMPLE CONDITIONING
23 • #7 COMPETITION AND A CONTRITE SPIRIT
25 • #8 HUMILITY AT THE FRONT OF THE PACK

LOVE: For whom do you care?

28 • #9 PLAYING WITH THE GREATEST MOTIVATION
30 • #10 LOVE—WHAT IS IT AND WHERE CAN IT BE
FOUND?
32 #11 CREDENTIALS OF A GOOD ASSISTANT COACH
34 • #12 FALLING IN LOVE WITH THE ONE
WHO LOVES YOU MOST

SEX AND DATING: What are your values?

38 • #13 "IF YOU LOVED ME, YOU'D . . ."
41 • #14 WAITING FOR THE "ALL-AMERICAN HUNK"
44 • #15 BREAKING UP WITHOUT CRACKING UP
46 • #16 WHEN THE STRONG ABUSE THE WEAK

FEMININITY: Are you a lady?

50 • #17 BECOMING A WORLD-CLASS LADY
52 • #18 A "MISS AMERICA" WITH MUSCLES?
55 • #19 "DIFFERENT STROKES FOR DIFFERENT FOLKS"
57 • #20 YOUR BEST POSITION

3

BAD HABITS: How does Satan try to trip you up?

60 • **#21** CONTROLLING THE MOST POWERFUL
MUSCLE IN THE BODY
62 • **#22** THE ROCK OF THIS WORLD
OR THE ROCK OF THE AGES?
65 • **#23** ONE WAY 2 PLAY
67 • **#24** TO EAT OR NOT TO EAT . . .

TOUGH TIMES: How do you handle problems?

70• **#25** "SOMETIMES I FEEL LIKE
THE LONE RANGERETTE"
72 • **#26** "MY TEAMMATE DROPPED THE BALL
AND COACH YELLED AT ME!"
74 • **#27** WHEN YOU FEEL LIKE CHECKING
IN FOR KEEPS
76 • **#28** THE ANTIDOTE FOR STRESS

RECOVERY: What if you've fallen?

80 • **#29** WHEN THE PAST HINDERS YOUR FUTURE
82 • **#30** WOUNDED ON THE INSIDE
85 • **#31** PICKING UP THE PIECES
87 • **#32** RUNNING TO WIN

APPENDICES

89 • **Appendix I** • THE WINNING RUN
93 • **Appendix II** • A BALLPLAYER'S PARAPHRASE
of 1 Corinthians 13:1-8

IDENTITY

Who are You?

COMPETING ON THE ENEMY'S "HOME COURT"

Read Genesis 3

THE HOME COURT ADVANTAGE means much in a basketball game. The home team is accustomed to the background, the lights and the routine before the game. The home fans are usually more numerous and sometimes even the officials tend to give a home team the benefit of the doubt! Some coaches feel it's worth from eight to ten points just to be on one's own home court.

Christians are playing the game of life on the enemy's home court. This has been true ever since the fall of Adam and Eve in the Garden of Eden. God originally gave dominion of the earth to man.

> Then God said, "Let us make man in our image, in our likeness, and let them rule over the fish of the sea and the birds of the air, over the livestock, over all the earth, and over all the creatures that move along the ground."
> So God created man in his own image, in the image of God he created him; male and female he created them.
> God blessed them and said to them, "Be fruitful and increase in number; fill the earth and subdue it. Rule over the fish of the sea and the birds of the air and over every living creature that moves on the ground."
> Then God said, "I give you every seed bearing plant on the face of the whole earth and every tree that has fruit with seed in it. They will be yours for food. And to all the beasts of the earth and all the birds of the air and all the creatures that move on the ground—everything that has the breath of life in it—I give every green plant for food." And it was so.
> Genesis 1:26-30

When Adam and Eve followed Satan instead of obeying the Lord they gave that authority to the devil.

6

To Adam he (God) said, "Because you listened to your wife and ate from the tree about which I commanded you, 'You must not eat of it,' "Cursed is the ground because of you; through painful toil you will eat of it all the days of your life. It will produce thorns and thistles for you, and you will eat the plants of the field. By the sweat of your brow you will eat your food until you return to the ground, since from it you were taken; for dust you are and to dust you will return."

Genesis 3:17-19

Now Satan is the "ruler of the kingdom of the air," the "Spirit at work in those who are disobedient" (Ephesians 2:1-2). Though he has limited power, he has authority over all unsaved people, over all world systems, and over the fallen natures inside every man, woman, boy, and girl.

When a person trusts Christ as Savior, he or she becomes a new member of God's invisible Kingdom. This world is no longer our real home. That home is in heaven, and we eagerly await our Savior's return to take us there.

But our citizenship is in heaven. And we eagerly await a Savior from there, the Lord Jesus Christ, who by the power that enables him to bring everything under his control, will transform our lowly bodies so that they will be like his glorious body.

Philippians 3:20-21

As believers, our values differ from those of unbelievers. We don't measure ourselves by the same standards anymore. The great Apostle Paul wrote,

I beg you when I come I may not have to be as bold as I expect to be toward some people who think that we live by the standards of this world. For though we live in the world, we do not wage war as the world does. The weapons we fight with are not the weapons of the world. On the contrary, they have divine power to demolish strongholds. We demolish arguments and every pretension that sets itself up against the knowledge of God, and we take captive every thought to make it obedient to Christ.

2 Corinthians 10:2-5

7

We get our marching orders not from majority vote, popular opinion, or traditions of men, but from God's Word. Our power comes not from self, but from the Holy Spirit who lives within us. There is no good in our old sinful nature and no power in the new nature we have been given. That's why we must constantly rely on God's Spirit to empower us.

Because of Satan, we must play the game of life with alertness and self-control.

> Be self-controlled and alert. Your enemy the devil prowls around like a roaring lion looking for someone to devour. Resist him, standing firm in the faith, because you know that your brothers throughout the world are undergoing the same kind of sufferings.
>
> 1 Peter 5:8-9

We must count ourselves dead to self because of our old sinful nature.

> For we know that our old self was crucified with him so that the body of sin might be done away with, that we should no longer be slaves to sin—because anyone who has died has been freed from sin.
>
> In the same way, count yourselves dead to sin but alive to God in Christ Jesus. Therefore do not let sin reign in your mortal body so that you obey its evil desires. Do not offer the parts of your body to sin, as instruments of wickedness, but rather offer yourselves to God, as those who have been brought from death to life; and offer the parts of your body to him as instruments of righteousness. For sin shall not be your master, because you are not under law, but under grace.
>
> Romans 6:6-7, 11-14

And we must remember that the systems of this world— its ideas, its tastes, its influences— are never towards God. We are on the enemy's home court throughout life.

THINK IT OVER

How do your values and standards differ from those of unbelievers in Jesus?

FOCUS ON THE FINISH LINE

Memorize 1 John 2:15:

Do not love the world or anything in the world. If anyone loves the world, the love of the Father is not in him.

8

WHEN YOUR PRACTICE DOESN'T MATCH YOUR POSITION

Read Colossians 1

NADIA COMANECI, a 15-year-old Romanian gymnast, was expected to be a tough competitor in the 1976 Olympics. But no one expected her to be perfect. Yet, the judges could find no flaws in her balance beam routine and she was awarded the first perfect score of "10" in Olympic history! But Nadia wasn't through yet. She stunned the world of sports with three more "10's" on the balance beam and then an astounding four more perfect marks on the uneven parallel bars! In becoming the women's all-around champion, Nadia had become world-famous for her perfect performances!

While Nadia may have performed with perfection from man's viewpoint, her physical performance is not nearly as important as the way we perform on the spiritual "balance beam of life." There is much misunderstanding which leads to wrong emphases on this subject. What does God say about our position in Christ and about our performance? He has both good news and bad news for us.

First, as believers we are rescued from Satan's kingdom and placed into the kingdom of Christ.

> For he has rescued us from the dominion of darkness and brought us into the kingdom of the Son he loves, in whom we have redemption, the forgiveness of sins.
>
> Colossians 1:13-14

Before we were saved, we were condemned.

> Whoever believes in him is not condemned, but whoever does not believe stands condemned already because he has not believed in the name of God's one and only Son.
>
> John 3:18

9

We were lost.

The Son of Man came to save what was lost.

Matthew 18:11

And even if our gospel is veiled, it is veiled to those who are perishing. The god of this age has blinded the minds of unbelievers, so that they cannot see the light of the gospel of the glory of Christ, who is the image of God.

2 Corinthians 4:3-4

We were guilty.

Now we know that whatever the law says, it says to those who are under the law, so that every mouth may be silenced and the whole world held accountable to God.

Romans 3:19

We were spiritually dead and children of wrath.

As for you, you were dead in your transgressions and sins, in which you used to live when you followed the ways of this world and of the ruler of the kingdom of the air, the spirit who is now at work in those who are disobedient. All of us also lived among them at one time, gratifying the cravings of our sinful nature and following its desires and thoughts. Like the rest, we were by nature objects of wrath. But because of his great love for us, God, who is rich in mercy, made us alive with Christ even when we were dead in transgressions — it is by grace you have been saved.

Ephesians 2:1-5

We were alienated from God.

They are darkened in their understanding and separated from the life of God because of the ignorance that is in them due to the hardening of their hearts.

Ephesians 4:1

We were enemies of God.

For if, when we were God's enemies, we were reconciled to him through the death of his Son, how much more, having been reconciled, shall we be saved through his life.

Romans 5:10

Once you were alienated from God and were enemies in your minds because of your evil behavior.

Colossians 1:21

BUT WHEN WE TRUSTED CHRIST, we obtained redemption and forgiveness of every sin.

For he has rescued us from the dominion of darkness and brought us into the kingdom of the Son he loves, in whom we have redemption, the forgiveness of sins.

Colossians 1:13-14

We were reconciled to God and destined to be presented holy and blameless in His sight.

But now he has reconciled you by Christ's physical body through death to present you holy in his sight, without blemish and free from accusation . . . .

Colossians 1:22

We are predestined to be adopted as sons.

In love, he predestined us to be adopted as his sons through Jesus Christ, in accordance with his pleasure and will, which he has freely given us in the One he loves.

Ephesians 1:5-6

We are also predestined to be conformed to His image.

For those God foreknew he also predestined to be conformed to the likeness of his Son, that he might be the firstborn among many brothers.

Romans 8:29

We now have the very righteousness of Christ accounted to us before God!

God made him who had no sin to be sin for us, so that in him we might become the righteousness of God.

2 Corinthians 5:21

We are eternally secure in this position, for God did not promise us all this and then put us on probation! In other words, positionally He sees us as perfect because of the righteousness of Jesus Christ imputed to us! Our sins are not counted against us.

> . . . that God was reconciling the world to himself in Christ, not counting men's sins against them.
>
> 2 Corinthians 5:10

But they were charged to Christ's account! In position, we are more perfect than Nadia on the balance beam! What a reason to praise God!

On the other side of the coin, we still sin and fall short in daily practice. We will not be perfect "10's" until we get to Heaven! Because of the sinful nature which trips us up, we must constantly fight against sin. When we sin, we hate it. Then we must agree with God that we have sinned (confess) and trust His forgiveness. We needn't compare ourselves with others or to our own expectations, or we are sure to be discouraged. A good self-image depends not upon how we see ourselves, but upon seeing Him! As we keep our eyes upon Jesus, our performances will more closely match our position. We will bear fruit and grow in knowledge of Him, being strengthened with the supernatural power of God.

> And we pray this in order that you may live a life worthy of the Lord and may please him in every way: bearing fruit in every good work, growing in the knowledge of God, being strengthened with all power according to his glorious might so that you may have great endurance and patience, and joyfully giving thanks to the Father, who has qualified you to share in the inheritance of the saints in the kingdom of light.
>
> Colossians 1:10-12

Victory is assured, for one day we will be presented perfect ("complete" or "mature") in Christ!

> We proclaim him, admonishing and teaching everyone with all wisdom, so that we may present everyone perfect in Christ.
>
> Colossians 1:28

THINK IT OVER

Meditate upon the position you have been given in Christ. How, in practice, is your performance affected by this position?

12

FOCUS ON THE FINISH LINE

Memorize Colossians 1:28:

We proclaim Him, admonishing and teaching everyone with all wisdom, so that we may present everyone perfect in Christ.

A HEALTHY SELF-IMAGE

Read 2 Corinthians 5:11-21

DOT RICHARDSON had been an outstanding softball player before becoming a surgeon in California.. When women's softball was added to the Olympics for 1996, she made the USA team and fulfilled a dream by hitting a home run in her first Olympic game! Then, the shortstop-surgeon hit another one to win the Gold Medal!

Dot Richardson had visualized success before she ever attained it. Likewise, the mental picture you have of yourself ("self-image") has much to do with determining your capability in life. You'll never achieve all you are capable of until you think positively about yourself. Until you think positively about yourself, your attitude toward God will not be good, for you will blame Him for the failure you think you are!

All of us are sinners, but our sin and our person are different entities. We are to despise our sin and our selfish tendency toward sin, while we must love ourselves as we love others. To think we must hate ourselves is to hold an erroneous view of Scripture.

The monsters of inferiority and insecurity are big ones—but not bigger than God. No problem is big to an omnipotent God! In reality, all of us are insecure within ourselves. We only differ in how we handle our problems. Studies show that 80 percent of American teens dislike something about their appearance. Even Farrah Fawcett-Majors once confided that she felt her mouth was too large! Inevitable skin problems caused by active oil glands in adolescence, the lack of a closet full of designer clothes like some of our peers, or falling short of our own expectations in athletics lead some of us to feelings of inferiority. Remember—teen years pass quickly and the skin problems will become only a dim memory! So will the popularity problem, for the society you are part of will never again be assembled as now. If you base feelings about yourself on popularity, you will lose it immediately after high school graduation! Accept with gratitude the things you cannot change about yourself. Thank God for whatever degree of success He has given you in sports, for God accepts us regardless of our performance! He made you and He has gifted you in certain areas. It may help to visit with a trusted Christian teacher or friend to help identify your strengths. She probably has faced and conquered the same problems you are facing! Maximize what you do well. As you throw yourself into the area of your gifts, you will find new meaning each day.

No matter how you feel, what you've done, or what has happened to you, Jesus Christ knows and understands. He will never leave or forsake you.

> Keep your lives free from the love of money and be content
> with what you have, because God has said, "Never will I
> leave you; never will I forsake you."
> Hebrews 13:5 (quoting Deuteronomy 31:6)

He not only has the answer to problems, He IS the answer. Receive Him as your Savior and Lord. Then study God's attitude toward you. He says you are a new creature, reconciled to God, an ambassador of Christ, and the very righteousness of God! He deeply loves you with a love you cannot earn—so don't try! As you share His love with someone else, your self-image will be transformed!

THINK IT OVER

Upon what do you base your self-image? Is it based upon looks or achievements? Or is it based upon what God says about you and how much He loves you?

FOCUS ON THE FINISH LINE

Memorize 2 Corinthians 5:17:
Therefore, if anyone is in Christ, he is a new creation, the old has gone, the new has come!

ROLE MODELS—
IT TAKES ONE
TO BECOME ONE

Read Philippians 3:17-21

ROBYN DOUBLASS is a 5'7" blonde basketball magician who criss-crosses America with her "Spin It" show. She shares her faith in Christ as she entertains crowds by spinning up to ten basketballs at once! Not long ago she was in elementary school watching the world's greatest female ball handler, Tanya Crevier, perform similar feats. "I sat there with wide eyes, thinking, Wow, I want to be able to do that," says Robyn. She practiced up to four hours a day, wrote to Tanya, and received encouragement from her role model. "At that age, I was probably eager to follow anybody and I got a positive role model," she says.

You are a role model to someone else. Athletes especially have a great effect on younger athletes. They need someone to follow. That's one reason it is so important to walk a straight and narrow path. Someone is watching and wanting to be just like you! We are role models whether we want to be or not. The only question is, "What type of role model are you?—a good one or a bad one?"

While we are role models, we need role models ourselves. It is vital to choose positive role models. Certainly the world is full of poor role models. Madonna has millions of fans, but she has been a poor role model. Lewd behavior, rebellion, and having a baby out of wedlock are poor examples for young fans. We need role models who will spur us toward righteousness. We need folks who show us it is possible to live moral lives, love parents, respect teachers and coaches, and seek God. Do you have such a model? Are you one yourself?

THINK IT OVER
Who is your role model of Godly living?

FOCUS ON THE FINISH LINE
Memorize Philippians 3:17:
Join with others in following my example, brothers, and take note of those who live according to the pattern we gave you.

ATTITUDE

What do you think?

LISTENING
TO THE RIGHT
VOICES

Read Luke 9:28-36

A HIGH SCHOOL BASKETBALL COACH became frustrated
because she was afraid that her team wasn't listening to her
instructions. So, during a time-out, the coach gathered the
team around her, looked into their eyes and mouthed words
without a sound! The crowd was cheering in the background
as the players focused upon their coach, nodding enthusiasti-
cally. Then they went back onto the court and did the same
things as before! The coach had proven her suspicions!

Sometimes we listen to our Heavenly Father about as
well as the basketball team listened to the coach. We spend so
much time running to functions that we don't take time to
listen to God. We say that one of our biggest problems is our
lack of time. But if we *took* time to listen to God, we'd *have*
time to do what is really important. We'd know His will for us
and wouldn't waste time on the things that won't last anyway!
Why won't we take time to listen to Him? Because we really
don't love Him as much as we love other pursuits! Studies
show that, on the average, we spend nineteen times more
hours watching TV than we spend in Sunday School. Through
the influence of radio, TV, movies, magazines, and music, we
have become addicted to the voices of this world. These voices
threaten the vitality of our walk with God.

Overexposure to TV is dangerous because it beams the
world's value system into our brain—a sensitive computer
that consciously or subconsciously stores every bit of information ever fed into it. To put it simply, we program our
very lives. We become what our mind dwells upon. And most
of the information on television is not coming from God's
perspective! But that's not the only danger. TV addicts become
less creative and more passive. Our entire potential is sapped
when we vegetate in front of the tube! It is not possible to fill

our minds with hours of television or worldly movies and to maintain zest and vitality in our walk with God. We *must* listen to Him.

> A voice came from the cloud, saying, "This is my Son, whom I have chosen; listen to him."
>
> Luke 5:35

What about the music we allow to fill our stereos and car radios? Rock music becomes an addiction to many of us. But the basic theme, even the reason for its existence, is to promote illicit sex, drugs, rebellion, and the occult. You cannot walk with God while filling your mind with Satan's lyrics.

Satan also uses magazines and billboards to keep our minds from God. He uses these to encourage materialism, lust, and greed. If we would keep our thoughts pure, we must keep our eyes off his allurements.

Sounds pretty radical, huh? In this sense, our Lord Jesus was also radical! But God provided for all His needs as He completed His radical mission. He promises to do the same for you. You'll know His mind as you spend quality time with God. As you listen to His voice, you'll think His thoughts and your life will bring much praise to your Heavenly Father.

THINK IT OVER

What habits must you develop and what must you avoid if you are to hear the voice of God and dwell upon good things.

FOCUS ON THE FINISH LINE

Memorize Philippians 4:8:

Finally, brothers, whatever is true, whatever is noble, whatever is right, whatever is pure, whatever is lovely, whatever is admirable—if anything is excellent or praiseworthy—think about such things.

TEMPLE
CONDITIONING

Read 1 Corinthians 3:16-17

WHEN THE PEOPLE OF GOD built His temple during the reign of Solomon, it was under the specific direction of the Creator Himself. The pre-cut foundation stones fit perfectly and the inner walls were paneled with cedar and overlaid in gold. The glory of God came down and dwelt in this wonder of the ancient world!

Today God does not dwell in temples made with human hands.

> The God who made the world and everything in it is the Lord of heaven and earth and does not live in temples built by hands.
>
> Acts 17:24

Rather, He indwells the physical body of those who trust His Son, the Lord Jesus Christ, as their personal Savior. Phenomenal! When I received Jesus, the Spirit of the God of this universe dwelt in this body!

Since we do not own this physical body, we must be sure it is kept in the best condition for our Master's use. Among other things, this means that regular physical exercise is part of the spiritual worship due our Creator.

> Therefore, I urge you, brothers, in view of God's mercy, to offer your bodies as living sacrifices, holy and pleasing to God — this is your spiritual act of worship.
>
> Romans 12:1

Optimal frequency, intensity and duration varies for each individual and it is our responsibility to discover that which is best for our height, weight, and age. Spiritual discipline is then required to maintain physical fitness. Some wrongly believe that physical condition can be neglected while every-thing is okay spiritually." But is uncontrolled eating really any less a sin than drunkenness? Or adultery? Or stealing? Certainly, all sins are ugly in God's sight.

Approximately thirty physiological reasons why physical conditioning is beneficial to God's temple could be listed. Suffice it to say that the heart and respiratory system become more efficient (laboring less to do the same amount of work), undesirable fat deposits in the blood and in other areas of the body are eliminated, protective proteins in blood are increased, and the body becomes more resistant to disease and stress. Needless to say, the conditioned individual feels better, has less sickness, looks better, and has more endurance to meet his daily demands. How many Christians have not become all that God wanted them to be because of unfaithful stewardship of the physical body?

Are you convinced you must condition God's temple as a steward of the grace of God? Do you know you must condition yourself also in consideration of others? Obesity can be a stumbling block to someone with whom you may want to share the gospel. An undisciplined lifestyle may hinder some-one else from finding the Savior. Do you think Jesus was overweight? Of course not! Then why should any of His servants be obese? Are you married? Your body belongs to your spouse.

> The husband should fulfill his marital duty to his wife, and likewise the wife to her husband. The wife's body does not belong to her alone but also to her husband. In the same way, the husband's body does not belong to him alone but also to his wife.
>
> 1 Corinthians 7:4-5

You are grossly inconsiderate if you do nothing about an overweight problem. Did you know your mate is primarily stimulated visually? You may be ruining your sexual relationship with your own husband. When that happens, marriage problems are inevitable.

There is nothing evil about the physical body! Though we suffer because the effects of sin have caused weakness, the body itself is not evil. It's easy to see why many people who believe the body to be evil have severe self-image problems! Our bodies were created by God as a temple for His

Spirit. He made us each in unique fashion. We should thank and praise Him for His wisdom in their design and glorify Him by maintaining them to the maximum.

Someone says, "bodily exercise profits little" (1 Timothy 4:8). That's true, and we should want all the profit available for the glory of God! Many Christians deny their responsibility toward God's temple by quoting this verse because they really don't want to discipline themselves. As children of the Living God, we are to love and care for our bodies.

> In this same way, husbands ought to love their wives as their own bodies. He who loves his wife loves himself. After all, no one ever hated his own body, but he feeds and cares for it, just as Christ does the church . . .
>
> Ephesians 5:28-29

Discipline in physical exercise is indispensable.

The human body was designed by God for motion. Even for those who are not obese, a sedentary lifestyle is contrary to what is best for health. Our example in physical fitness, as in every area, is the Lord Jesus Himself. Though He could have ridden up and down Palestine on the best Arabian horse, He walked everywhere He went. Only once is it recorded that He rode, and that was on a donkey when He went into Jerusalem. Jesus not only worked physically as a carpenter when growing up, but He also remained a physically active person until He died on the cross for your sins and mine.

So let's go, ladies! Consult your doctor for a physical examination. Then begin a regular fitness program and stay with it!

THINK IT OVER

What is your attitude toward physical fitness? Are you committed to remaining fit for life?

FOCUS ON THE FINISH LINE

Memorize 1 Corinthians 3:16-17:

Don't you know that you yourselves are God's temple and that God's Spirit lives in you? If anyone destroys God's temple, God will destroy him; for God's temple is sacred, and you are that temple.

COMPETITION AND A CONTRITE SPIRIT

Hurdle # 7

Read 2 Timothy 2

WITH THE CURRENT STRESS upon aggression, success, and victory in our society, it is not easy to cope with finishing in less than first place, or to maintain a balance of aggressive competition and a gentle spirit. United States figure skater Rosalynn Summers' experience is an example. *USA Today* reported that it took her several months to recover from the disappointment of receiving a silver medal rather than a gold one in the 1984 Winter Olympics. She was quoted as saying, "the pressure had been built up for so long. The gold medal was right there . . . So anything less . . . would be a failure. When I didn't win the gold, I felt like a complete failure, and I didn't enjoy myself."

It is possible to reinforce both good and bad habits, both right and wrong values on the athletic field. The need to play aggressively to succeed in athletics can tempt us to develop a brash hardness and wrong priorities that are ungodly. There is great need for balance in our values and our spirits, for the Lord desires to develop a gentle, quiet spirit within each of His children.

Certainly, there is a time and place for a woman to be aggressive and assertive. If one's children are threatened, a godly woman is ready to lay down her life for them. We ought to be extremely angry with the sins of our society—the murder of innocent babies via abortion, the toleration of sexual promiscuity and homosexuality, and the exploitation of women through pornography. These evils ought to make our blood boil! We must aggressively oppose them!

But for those who marry, God has determined the female role to be one of support and help to her husband. Both husband and wife must maintain a soft heart towards the Lord and towards each other. That's where the danger

23

lies. While athletics and the aggressiveness they require is temporary, character is permanent. What do you desire your character to be like in ten years? What kind of mate do you desire? Do you want a leader of your family, or will you aggressively challenge his leadership every step of the way? You have a lot to say about whether you marry for "Heaven" or for "Hell".

> Better to live in a desert than with a quarrelsome and ill-tempered wife.
>
> Proverbs 21:19

> Better to live on a corner of the roof than share a house with a quarrelsome wife.
>
> Proverbs 25:24

There is a saying that says:
Sow a thought, reap an action.
Sow an action, reap a habit.
Sow a habit, reap a destiny.
What kinds of thoughts, actions, and habits are you sowing on the athletic field? Your character will be determined by your habits now. Stay in the Word of God, and let His Spirit talk to you about this dilemma. Listen to Him and He will make His plans clear for your life.

THINK IT OVER
What can you do to maintain a gentle spirit and the right priorities while competing aggressively in athletics?

FOCUS ON THE FINISH LINE
Memorize 2 Timothy 1:7:
For God did not give us a spirit of timidity, but a spirit of power, of love and of self-discipline.

HUMILITY
AT THE FRONT
OF THE PACK

Hurdle #8

Read Philippians 2:1-13

BABE DIDRIKSEN ZAHARIAS was already an All-American
basketball player when she suddenly became a national track
and field star. On July 4, 1932, she entered the Women's AAU
Championships on the campus of Northwestern University
and won the *team* title by scoring thirty points herself! Of the
eight events she entered, she won six of them, setting world
records in the 80-meter hurdles, the javelin, and the high
jump! In second place was the University of Illinois, which
sent twenty-two women to the meet and scored twenty-two
points.

At the 1932 Los Angeles Olympics, Babe irritated her
teammates by boasting, "I am out to beat everybody in sight,
and that's just what I'm going to do." What happened? She set
new world records in every event she entered—the javelin, the
80-meter hurdles and the high jump!

Babe became a celebrity overnight, touring with the
House of David baseball team and even pitching an inning for
the St. Louis Cardinals in an exhibition game. Then, golf
became her greatest success. She became the greatest woman
golfer in the world, winning fourteen straight tournaments
from 1946-1947. She was the first American woman to win
the British Amateur Open. Before she died in 1956, she was
voted the greatest female athlete of the half century.

Success as the great Babe Zaharias experienced
always presents a temptation to become proud. In a sense,
the success is a real trial to be overcome, for only by recogniz-
ing our inadequacy do we realize God's sufficiency. The worst
use that can be made of success is to boast of it! And the
more we think about humility, the more elusive humility
becomes!

What is humility? It is not thinking less of yourself—it
is just not thinking of yourself! It is not a drooping, dragging
appearance, acting "lower than a snake's belly." It is not

25

thinking you are no good and can never do anything right. Humility is seeing yourself as God sees you. As far as merit in earning salvation, we are lost and bankrupt sinners. But, because of His great love for you and me, God sent Jesus to die for us! In His mercy, He decided that we were worth saving. He paid the very life of His Son for our redemption! The fact that Jesus died for us is the source of our true self-worth! Not that we deserve it, but that He did it anyway!

Therefore, no matter how much worldly success or failure we experience, by the power of God's Holy Spirit we can have the mind of Jesus — the mind of a servant of God.

> Your attitude should be the same as that of Christ Jesus: Who, being in very nature God, did not consider equality with God something to be grasped, but made himself nothing, taking the very nature of a servant, being made in human likeness. And being found in appearance as a man, he humbled himself and became obedient to death — even death on a cross! Therefore, God exalted him to the highest place and gave him the name that is above every name, that at the name of Jesus every knee should bow, in heaven and on earth and under the earth, and every tongue confess that Jesus Christ is Lord, to the glory of God the Father.
>
> Philippians 2:5-11

We realize that all success comes from God. In His sovereignty, He causes or allows it all. He has a purpose in your successes, as well as in your failures, and that purpose is for you to give glory to Him!

Never touch His glory by taking any of it for yourself! He is a very jealous God when it comes to His glory among His creatures. Give Him all the praise. He promises to exalt those who do so.

> Humble yourselves before the Lord, and he will lift you up.
>
> James 4:10

THINK IT OVER

How do both success and failure affect your attitude toward God? Toward yourself? Toward others? How should these things affect your attitude?

FOCUS ON THE FINISH LINE

Memorize Philippians 2:5-7:

Your attitude should be the same as that of Christ Jesus: Who, being in very nature God, did not consider equality with God something to be grasped, but made himself nothing, taking the very nature of a servant, being made in human likeness.

LOVE

For whom do you care?

PLAYING WITH
THE GREATEST
MOTIVATION

Hurdle #9

Read Colossians 3

MADELINE MANNING, a Tennessee State "Tigerbelle" from Cleveland, Ohio, was one of many great women sprinters from TSU to compete in the Olympic Games. Her time of 2:00.9 in the 800-meters set a new Olympic record in the 1968 Mexico City Games. In that race, Madeline was spurred on by a unique form of motivation. After shooting out to an early lead, she caught a whiff of the garlicky perspiration of one of the other runners and pulled away in the backstretch of the final lap. Madeline won by over 10 meters!

Each of us has a variety of motivations for doing what we do in life, but "garlicky perspiration" is a rare one! In sports, our motivation often comes from a coach or a parent, who assist by encouraging us to excel, to go beyond where we have gone before. Coaches do this by providing motives for a higher level of effort. In fact, the word "motivation" means "to incite to action," or "to provide with a reason" for action.

Sometimes we are driven to perform for the wrong reasons. Playing a game to attract the attention of a guy we'd like to date, or playing for personal glory are not valid motives for participation in athletics. Nor is playing because of the external pressures of society enough motivation to excel. Nor is playing to appear favorably in the eyes of others. In fact, the compulsion to appear physically attractive to others can become an obsession leading to severe problems. Many girls have desired such a trim physique that they become obsessed to do away with *any* fat and soon start seeing food as calories instead of nutrition. Severe eating disorders like anorexia or bulimia have then been spawned. Muscle actually weighs more than fat, so as these girls notice slight increases in body weight because of better muscle tone through exercise, panic sets in. They are not fat, but see themselves as fat! The mind says, "Cut calories to reduce weight." But they don't need to cut calories. The calories are needed for energy to perform!

Thus, a vicious cycle sets in, all because of trying to "appear" before others.

How much better to play not for selfish reasons, but for the glory of God because we love Him. If His glory is our only goal, the Lord Jesus Christ will be on our minds. He accepts us as we are, just as He made us. We don't have to "appear" a certain physique before others. We are to do whatever we do as unto Him. He is the motivation. He is the "incitement to action." We can visualize Him as our only audience and perform as unto the Lover of our soul. Any other motive is unfulfilling and even dangerous.

THINK IT OVER

What can you do each day to keep your mind on heavenly things and off of yourself or your performance?

FOCUS ON THE FINISH LINE

Memorize Colossians 3:23-24:

Whatever you do, work at it with all your heart, as working for the Lord, not for men, since you know that you will receive an inheritance from the Lord as a reward. It is the Lord Christ you are serving.

LOVE —
WHAT IS IT
AND WHERE
CAN IT BE FOUND?

Hurdle #10

Read 1 Corinthians 13

THE SPECIAL OLYMPICS provide many great opportunities to express love to the mentally handicapped. The finish line of each race is staffed by what the Olympians call "huggers." In addition to calling out the winners, the "huggers" are to encourage each contestant throughout the race and to welcome each one to the finish line with a hug and a pat on the back. It is well-known that people respond best to love, and these outward expressions serve to motivate the Special Olympians as well as they would anyone else!

These examples are too few and far between in a society which has a warped view of love. What is the real meaning of love? To answer that question, let's look at what love is *not.*

First, love is not a warm feeling. A loving God did not sit in heaven and have a warm feeling toward us when we rebelled in sin against Him. He took the initiative and sent His only Son to die for us! In fact, He loves you so personally and warmly that if you had been the only sinner on earth He would still have died for you! Real love involves action on the part of the lover.

Second, love is not empty words. "I love you," spoken to a girl by a young guy should cause red flags to go up in her mind. Often what he really means is, "I lust for your body." Those words can be not only a physical trap but a psychological trap as a girl feels a commitment has been made when a guy intends to make no permanent commitment. Girls are especially vulnerable if emotionally starved for affection and attention at home. Real love says, "Because I love you, I will have no sex with you or even arouse you physically until we are married." Staying together in marriage is partly based upon having no sex before marriage, for the resentment, regret and guilt of illicit sex pulls couples apart after marriage.

30

Third, love is not getting for oneself. Love is giving to bless others. Love has the other's best interests in mind. "For God so loved the world that He *gave*" (John 3:16). One who loves does not try to subject or dominate the loved one, but listens to, cares for, and respects the opinions of the beloved.

Now, what *is* love? Love is a matter of the will and the heart—not a matter of the eyes or the hormones. In a sense, love is blind. The lover chooses not to see the scars, bad habits, and other negatives in the beloved. You refuse to believe the beloved would deceive you and if he *really* loves you he won't deceive you. Yet the risk is always there!

Because God is love, the best place to find love is in godly people. Choose for your closest companions those who love and serve the Lord Jesus Christ. That's the place to find real love. And the friends who love Jesus will draw out the love of God in you, too!

THINK IT OVER

How can you recognize when someone really loves you? What are the best ways for you to show love to others?

FOCUS ON THE FINISH LINE
Memorize 1 John 4:7-8:

Dear friends, let us love one another, for love comes from God. Everyone who loves has been born of God and knows God. Whoever does not love does not know God, because God is love.

CREDENTIALS
OF A GOOD
ASSISTANT COACH

Hurdle #11

Read Proverbs 31

THERE IS GREAT FULFILLMENT in the coaching profession when two or more coaches work together fulfilling their roles on the team. A wise head coach is selective in choosing assistants, for they can make or break the program. A good assistant is enthusiastic, knowledgeable, reliable and understanding of the chain of command. Above all, a good assistant is loyal to the head coach. Assistant coaches have many opportunities to undermine or reinforce the desires of the head coach and loyalty is one quality that is not negotiable.

Marriage is a relationship that also requires a great deal of loyalty to make it a success. God has ordained a role relationship between man and woman. Before a girl says, "I do," she must be certain she can be loyal, submissive and obedient to her future husband. While each is equal in value to God, the wife is to be subject to the husband for two reasons. She is subject because Adam was created first. Also she is subject because it was Eve that was deceived.

> A woman should learn in quietness and full submission. I do not permit a woman to teach or to have authority over a man; she must be silent. For Adam was formed first, then Eve. And Adam was not the one deceived; it was the woman who was deceived and became a sinner. But women will be saved through childbearing — if they continue in faith, love and holiness with propriety.
>
> 1 Timothy 2:11-15

Adam, the head of the human race, *knowingly* disobeyed God and is responsible for the consequences. Eve was *deceived* by Satan.

A godly wife finds much joy in supporting her husband.

Wives, in the same way be submissive to your husbands so that, if any of them do not believe the word, they may be won over without words by the behavior of their wives, when they see the purity and reverence of your lives. Your beauty should not come from outward adornment, such as braided hair and the wearing of gold jewelry and fine clothes. Instead, it should be that of your inner self, the unfading beauty of a gentle and quiet spirit, which is of great worth in God's sight. For this is the way the holy women of the past who put their hope in God used to make themselves beautiful. They were submissive to their own husbands, like Sarah, who obeyed Abraham and called him her master. You are her daughters if you do what is right and do not give way to fear.

1 Peter 3:1-6

The call of God to being a wife and mother is a high calling. It is to be more important than a woman's career—or she should not marry in the first place. While working outside the home is not prohibited in Scripture, there are many possible dangers. The working wife often gives many of her best hours to another authority. She is pressured to neglect her first calling as wife and mother, and may become competitive in marriage. It becomes a temptation to reverse her God-appointed role with that of her husband. Her loyalties can easily become divided.

The subordinate role is really the easiest to fulfill! While the head coach makes the decisions (with counsel from the subordinate), *he* is responsible. If they fail, he takes the heat! That's why a godly man listens to the input of a godly wife. He knows he needs all of her support and wise counsel.

THINK IT OVER

How can you prepare now to become the loyal "assistant" to your future husband?

FOCUS ON THE FINISH LINE

Memorize Proverbs 31:30:

Charm is deceptive, and beauty is fleeting; but a woman who fears the Lord is to be praised.

FALLING IN LOVE
WITH THE ONE
WHO LOVES YOU MOST

Hurdle #12

Read 1 John 4:7-21

EARLY IN HER CAREER, Amy Grant recalled her freshman
year at Furman University during a live concert. "It seemed to
me my freshman year we didn't worry so much about who we
were as who we knew. That was supposed to make you really
somebody. You know my sister once sat next to Barbara
Streisand on a plane—it kind of changed my life! I wasn't
there, but I kinda felt it. There was this girl who went to my
high school, she really got famous, yeah, she has paintings in
a New York Art gallery. It's not quite a famous New York art
gallery, but she's up there! She's in New York and she came
out of Tennessee—she went to *my* school! And a guy I knew
played professional football. He was only on the specialty
team, but he was on the team. Yeah! You know I knew somebody else who was in a play once off Broadway. I knew somebody else who was a co-pilot of a big jumbo jet. I sat on the
same plane that Dolly Parton sat on. She was a first row, first
class, and I was a first row, coach. Almost next door neighbors!
Isn't life ridiculous?! We meet somebody special and we feel like
Ooh—I'm different! Their blood must pump differently from my
blood and now that I've met them, I'll never be the same."

Why is it that so many people who say they know
Jesus don't value their friendship, their association with Him
as much as they seem to esteem other humans who may be
famous? If we could fall in love with the One who loves us
more than anyone else loves us, many of our problems would
be solved and our decisions made. What does it take for us to
fall in love with Jesus? We must remember He is the One who
loved us enough to die for us. No one else did that. We must
determine to be loyal to Jesus no matter what happens and
no matter what others think. You can think about Jesus day
and night, remembering special times you've had with Him.
Imagine what He is doing right now. Learn what Jesus likes

34

and dislikes and do the things He likes. Keep things that remind you of Him.

Talk to Jesus every chance you get and listen for His voice. Remember what he says to you by writing it down. Give Him your full attention often. Trust Him with the secrets of your heart. Do little creative things that you know will please Him. Look for ways to bring Jesus into your conversations and be excited when you talk about Him. Tell others about His character and His achievements. Defend Him to all who reject and slander Him. Explain that they wouldn't want to talk that way if they only knew Him. Tell them they have misjudged His great love for them and His awesome power. Report the good things Jesus had done for you. Have your appearance the way He likes for you to look. Wear the clothes He says are becoming to you as His personal representative. Put His gifts to you in prominent places, carry love letters from Him, and crave more time with Him. Finally, assure Him that you will always be faithful to Him. Fulfill that promise by your actions.

THINK IT OVER

Do you really love Jesus? Tell Him exactly how you feel. Ask Him to give you more love for Him each day.

FOCUS ON THE FINISH LINE

Memorize 1 John 4:19:

We love because He first loved us.

SEX AND DATING

What are your values?

"IF YOU LOVED ME, YOU'D . . ."

Read 1 Corinthians 6:9-20

IN THE WOMEN'S 440 METER RELAYS of the 1936 Olympics, the German girls were under intense pressure to perform. Adolf Hitler wanted to prove his theory of racial superiority and his girls had established a new world record in the semifinal heat. But the Americans had been only .7 second slower in their heat and featured Helen Stephens, the fastest woman in the world. The German strategy for the finals was to lead with their three fastest girls and guild up such a lead that not even Helen Stephens could overcome it. The third German runner had an 8-meter lead when she passed the baton to a nervous Ilse Dorffeldt for the final leg. With the pressure of the world's fastest runner coming from behind and the eyes of a world dictator in the stands, Ilse reached for the baton and grabbed only air. Then the baton slipped through her panic-stricken hands as she began her sprint. The hopes of a German victory fell to the ground with that baton.

Sometimes a boyfriend we really admire will place such pressure upon us to "perform" for him, that it would be easy to get our eyes off the Lord and "drop the baton" of moral purity. Many girls have fallen prey to this pressure and their lives have been shipwrecked as a result. They have been "defrauded" by men who have aroused desires that they could not righteously satisfy. In her desire for security, attention, and a caring relationship, the girl often falls victim to a guy looking only for sexual gratification. He can use sweet words like "I love you" to cover his real motive of "I lust for your body." When it's over, he departs and the girl keeps a part of him and possibly his baby! Now, *she* has given herself to someone with whom she has no permanent, binding relationship. She becomes a used person. If pregnant, does she drop out of school to have the baby? If so, who will support her and the child? If not, should she get an abortion? If so, she faces the guilt of the murder of the innocent baby, possible difficulty in conceiving again, difficulty in ever loving a child she could conceive, and depression over the killing. Millions have suffered tragically from lack of moral discipline in the area of sex. One girl wrote the following letter to a counselor:

> "I'm so ashamed to even tell you this, but I need help so badly. I cared so much for Bill and the first time he kissed me I thought he was the most wonderful guy in the world. We began spending more and more time kissing which led to petting and then when that got old we went all the way. I ended up telling him that our relationship was wrong and he told me in these exact words, 'I guess I should have been more honest with you, too. I loved you more as a friend than as a girlfriend.' Joe, I could have died! It tore me up! All that I had given him, thrown back in my face, like trash. It was so awful. I left before I started crying. I wasn't going to give him the satisfaction of seeing me cry. But on the way home, I was crying so hard. I felt so used and I felt like trash. He wasn't even my friend either. Friends don't lie to each other."

Another girl, thirteen years old, said this about her premarital experience, "I felt as if my insides were being exposed and my heart left unattended."

Contrary to the current attitudes of society, everyone is *not* "doing it." If a guy really loves you, he'll give you his name *before* the marriage act or even sexual arousal caused by "petting" takes place. If you give him sex, you will surely lose his respect and admiration. If he refuses to continue to date you because you won't "go all the way" you are much better off. You have discovered his real motive before giving up your purity.

What are some keys to overcoming this tremendous pressure? First, feed your mind on God's Word daily. Let the encouragement of the Lord replace the constant preoccupation with sexual thoughts. Second, stay out of potentially dangerous situations. Being alone with a boyfriend for extended periods of time at home or in a car are "hazardous conditions." Take God's Word along on dates and place it between the two of you if necessary! If he is offended by God's Word, you're better off without him! Avoid "teasing" a boy with suggestive clothes, statements, looks, or passionate kisses. Most guys just cannot handle these things, and their eyes and hands will go as far as you allow. Keep his hands off God's private property! Finally, "devote yourself to prayer " (Colossians 4:2). There is great power in both the Word of God and prayer.

THINK IT OVER

How can you keep a fresh vision of God which will empower you to say "no" to sexual pressures?

FOCUS ON THE FINISH LINE

Memorize 1 Corinthians 6:19-20:

Do you not know that your body is a temple of the Holy Spirit, who is in you, whom you have received from God? You are not your own; you were bought at a price. Therefore honor God with your body.

WAITING FOR THE "ALL AMERICAN HUNK"

Hurdle #14

Read Genesis 2

AT AGE EIGHT, a dream was born in the heart of Mary Lou Retton as she watched Romanian gymnast Nadia Comaneci perform in the Olympics. At twelve, Mary Lou quit other sports to channel her energies into gymnastics. At fourteen, she moved to Houston to train under Bela Karolyi, the great gymnastics coach who had fled communism to find freedom in America. For eighteen months, she trained 6-8 hours per day preparing for the 1984 Olympics. Her performances in those games captured the imagination of the entire country.

"The Lord is #1 for sure to me. There's no way I could live without Him in my life," said Mary Lou, who grew close to Jesus Christ through the peril of a knee injury only six weeks prior to the Olympics. During her teen years, Mary Lou dated a University of Texas football player named Shannon Kelley. "Shannon brings me closer to Christ. He's so open about his relationship with the Lord. I like that about him. I don't know what's out there for me. But I want to get married someday and have a big family," she says. "When that time comes I want to always be home when my kids come home. Just like my mom was for me."

God has placed within the heart of both man and woman the desire for each other. This is as true for others as it is for Mary Lou and Shannon. God has said that "it is not good that we be alone" (Genesis 2:18). The sexes compliment one another. The woman has a desire for the security of a home and the fulfillment of children. The man needs a "helpmeet." Stories of how the two have gotten together have made for romantic thrillers throughout history. But unfortunately, there is a trend toward the breakup of marriages in America today, and in some areas one out of two marriages end in divorce. Understanding the God-given desire for companionship and the heartache people have brought upon one

41

another, what traits should a Christian girl seek in a partner? What traits is a godly man seeking in a woman? Your answers to these questions will determine whom you will date!

First of all, what is the purpose of dating? For some people, it is just to have a good time together. But realistically, dating is a test of compatibility. It is an opportunity to determine whether two people even like each other. It is a search for a possible marriage partner, whether each realizes it or not.

A dating relationship is important, but until there is a vow of marriage it is not permanent. It requires real discernment to be involved with a steady date while participating athletically. You will have to make many decisions concerning priorities. But after the wedding day your marriage becomes second in importance only to your relationship to Christ. A career, a team, a job, a hobby all must fall behind marriage in priority. Therefore, it is important to think through what you want in a guy. For the Christian, it is absolutely essential to date only those who are committed to Jesus Christ. They are the only valid marriage partners.

> Do not be yoked together with unbelievers. For what do righteousness and wickedness have in common? Or what fellowship can light have with darkness? What harmony is there between Christ and Belial? What does a believer have in common with an unbeliever? What agreement is there between the temple of God and idols? For we are the temple of the living God. As God has said, "I will be their God, and they will be my people." "Therefore come out from them and be separate, says the Lord. Touch no unclean thing, and I will receive you." "I will be a Father to you, and you will be my sons and daughters, says the Lord Almighty."
>
> 2 Corinthians 6:14-18

The theory of "maybe he'll change when we're married" has brought utter ruin to the lives of many girls.

Where will you find such a guy? He certainly won't be found in the bars or at the wild parties! You'll only court trouble by looking there. In fact, it is best to wait for a godly man to find you. Girls who call guys and pursue the relationship often get hurt and usually lose the guy besides. Let him be the initiator. More than likely, God's man is frequenting the church, Fellowship of Christian Athletes meetings, and retreats. He is seeking to know God better. Both of you must love God and want to serve Him, for if you won't love God, you can't love each other!

Get yourself mentally and emotionally healthy before considering marriage. Then find someone who is a lot like yourself. Research shows that similarities are like "money in the bank" while differences are liabilities in a marriage. Finally, wait for the right time to marry. God always gives the best to those who wait!

THINK IT OVER

What traits do you want in a man and where are you most likely to find such a person?

FOCUS ON THE FINISH LINE

Memorize 2 Corinthians 6:14:

Do not be yoked together with unbelievers. For what do righteousness and wickedness have in common? Or what fellowship can light have with darkness?

BREAKING UP
WITHOUT
CRACKING UP

Read Philippians 4

WHILE THE "DATING GAME" is filled with highs and lows,
breaking up is definitely one of the low points. You may
endure some days feeling lower than the proverbial snake's
belly after a breakup! Yet, the feeling is not uncommon, for 50
percent of engagements fail to result in a marriage. Be assured, your shredded heart will mend and normalcy will
return. The hurt can be severe, especially if sex was involved,
but it may save even deeper heartache had you not broken up.
    What are some causes of breakups in the dating
game? One partner may move across the country, making a
continuing relationship impractical. Because all relationships
are progressive—you either grow closer together or further
apart—often this distance leads to a breakup. Any staleness
or sameness can itself cause one partner to seek another
steady. Constant bickering and fighting can result in breaking
up. Too much sexual temptation is another good reason to
break up and so are conflicting life goals and values. Sometimes two people realize they don't even like each other, but
have dated because the relationship has provided a false
sense of security. Age differences can result in breakups,
because the younger person is at the disadvantage of having
to grow up too fast. How sad to make two people miserable
because of trying to avoid the temporary pain of parting
company.
    What is the Christ-like attitude when you must tell a
steady date that you desire to "date around?" The Bible says
we must "speak the truth in love" (Ephesians 4:15). This
means we kindly, but honestly get to the point that the relationship is over. A balance of truth and love certainly will
require much prayer beforehand! Emphasize the worth of the
individual and the unfeasibility of the relationship as you see
it. Then stick with your decision, regardless of pleadings or
threats. Life is too short to nurse a relationship that has no
future.

What if your boyfriend desires to break up but you don't? Hurt city! But the wounds will heal. Crying is not wrong and can be cathartic. Moping around regretfully will not help you. Determine to forget the relationship and go on with your life.

> I can do everything through him who gives me strength.
> Philippians 4:13

It will help to turn off the whines and pines of numerous contemporary "love songs" during this time! Hold no bitterness, for it will eat you up.

> See to it that no one misses the grace of God and that no bitter root grows up to cause trouble and defile many.
> Hebrews 12:15

Avoid jumping quickly into a rebound relationship with someone else, for these cause more problems than they solve. Find your security in the Lord Jesus and grow more in love with Him. Remember others who are worse off—especially divorced people who felt "trapped" in a relationship and didn't have the courage to break a poor match before marriage! Your hurt is temporary and will heal in time. Someday you will be better able to help others with similar disappointments. Until then, thank God by faith that He is sovereignly controlling the events in your life.

THINK IT OVER

What is the good side of the break-up of your dating relationship? What advantages do you see ten years down the road? Do you believe God is faithfully controlling events in your life?

FOCUS ON THE FINISH LINE

Memorize Romans 8:28:

And we know that in all things God works for the good to those who love him, who have been called according to his purpose.

45

WHEN THE STRONG ABUSE THE WEAK

Hurdle #16

Read 1 Peter 3

THE SPORTS PAGES are filled with reports of star male athletes abusing wives or girlfriends. It has become so common, we are not shocked anymore. Many men seem to have turned to aggression against those who have meant the most to them.

God says that husbands are to be considerate of wives and are to respect them as the weaker partner. The implication is the same for boyfriends and girlfriends. Why do many women stay in abusive relationships when men ignore God's commands? The lack of a healthy relationship with a father causes some girls to seek love, acceptance, and approval from men who may take advantage of them. Sexual promiscuity and remaining in abusive relationships often results. Research shows that approximately one-third of teens in dating relationships endure some form of violence.

Women who stay in such relationships are hungry for love and attention. They overlook the pain, hoping things will improve. They don't want to tell friends because dating has become a status symbol and they don't want pressure to break up. Furthermore, they fear looking dumb to peers for staying in such a mess. They don't tell parents because they want their independence more than their own safety! Some have seen their mothers slapped around and therefore think abuse is acceptable. Most have such low self-esteem they somehow feel they deserve punishment. The most helpful thing to say to an abused friend is, "You don't deserve this." Try to help her feel good about herself. Don't put the guy down because she obviously likes him. Emphasize that she shouldn't accept verbal and physical abuse from anyone, however. She may fear "being alone" if she breaks up, so be a constant friend and companion. Abusers try to isolate wives/girlfriends from friends because they are jealous and controlling. Keep on being a friend. Often they use threats of violence to make women feel there is no way out, then use alcohol or drugs as an excuse for their abuse. They control people by intimidation.

Fleeing an abusive relationship may be the only solution. You were created in God's image and He loves you deeply. Your worth is centered in your relationship with Jesus Christ. Jesus is the answer to all self-image problems, peer pressures, and loneliness. Flee from abuse to Jesus and He will heal you both inside and outside!

THINK IT OVER

Why do some women stay in an abusive relationship?

FOCUS ON THE FINISH LINE

Memorize 1 Peter 3:12:

For the eyes of the Lord are on the righteous and his ears are attentive to their prayers, but the face of the Lord is against those who do evil.

FEMININITY

Are you a lady?

BECOMING A WORLD-CLASS LADY

Hurdle #17

Read 1 Timothy 2

AS A TEENAGER, Madeline Manning Mims broke all her school records. In her first major meet as a member of the Cleveland Track Club in 1966, she set a world-record in Toronto. She won the 800-meter run in the 1968 Mexico City Olympics. Madeline truly became a world-class athlete.

But Madeline also became a world-class lady.

"A lady," says Madeline, "is something you choose to be. All girls will grow up to be women. But a lady is someone who makes a choice to be a lady. She demands respect for herself as a lady and does not want to be treated like a male. The problem in women's sports is that some women try to get their identity as athletes by taking on and focusing on the masculine characteristics. They buy into a lie that says being masculine makes them better athletes.

"God created me as a woman and he created me as an athlete. As an athlete, I can be aggressive. I can become the best in the world in my sport, but I can also choose to be a lady. It's a misconception that you can't be both feminine and athletic at the same time."

Karen Drollinger, author of the book *Grace and Glory* about female athletes, describes it this way: "Femininity may not help a female athlete shoot free throws better, but accepting and fulfilling one's godly image gives her inner confidence to perform to the best of her ability. In other words, femininity is a necessity if women athletes are to be all that God created them to be."

Madeline's single mother raised her in a Cleveland ghetto. She modeled the positive character traits of perseverance, hard work, diligent study, faith in God, and femininity.

"I know a lot of women athletes who deny their femininity," says Madeline. "I've seen athletes destroy themselves by worshiping either their sport or themselves. For a woman athlete to think she has to be masculine basically says she doesn't know who she is. But when you get to know your Creator, then you start to know yourself. At that point, you have freedom because you no longer have to compromise your femininity or try to search for acceptance through your sport or by being masculine."

What is femininity? It's the way a lady dresses, talks, and walks. It's letting a man open a door for her to step through. It's fixing up one's hair and looking the best she can for the glory of God. It's not sexiness — that just means the person is a woman. It's being a real lady.

"The bottom line is your relationship with Christ," says Madeline. "If you don't know the God who created you, you won't be able to appreciate yourself as His creation."

THINK IT OVER

Does running, jumping and playing sports mean you are masculine, or simply that you are athletically gifted?

FOCUS ON THE FINISH

Memorize 1 Timothy 2:10:

. . . *but with good deeds, appropriate for women who profess to worship God.*

A "MISS AMERICA" WITH MUSCLES?

Hurdle #18

Read 1 Corinthians 9:24-27

FOUR-TIME ALL-AMERICAN LYNETTE WOODARD of Kansas scored an NCAA record, 3,649 points in her career. After her senior season, she was awarded The Wade Trophy as the best female collegiate player in America. In 1984 she was the captain and star of the gold medal winning U.S. Olympic team. Possibly her greatest achievement was becoming the first female member of the Harlem Globetrotters in 1985! Lynette has much to say about discipline. "Strive to conquer your body," she says. "For instance, if you don't like doing a particular running drill, and you know you have to do three repetitions at practice, discipline your body to do five or ten repetitions. Make your body your slave."

While there are some areas of life where one cannot "have her cake and eat it too," Lynette Woodard is proof that one can be both feminine and a great athlete. The female athlete can reflect the character of the Lord Jesus in appearance, in attitude, and in action. Let's examine some keys to representing Christ in all three areas.

In appearance, women need not worry about excessively bulky muscles while training. Sports psychologist Dorothy Harris reports that sixteen year-old Olympic swimmer Debby Meyer had her private doctor in California perform a chromosome evaluation . . . to reassure her that she hadn't "trained herself out of being a female." She needn't have worried, for females lack that capacity because of the absence of the male hormone, testosterone. Exercise will tone and strengthen, but rarely build bulk in girls. In dress, a girl can appear feminine and attractive, while still excelling on the athletic field. It is important to remember the advice of Jesus concerning appearance. He told us not to worry unduly about externals, but "to seek first the kingdom of God and His righteousness."

Therefore I tell you, do not worry about your life, what you will eat or drink; or about your body, what you will wear. Is not life more important than food, and the body more important than clothes? Look at the birds of the air; they do not sow or reap or store away in barns, and yet your heavenly Father feeds them. Are you not much more valuable than they? Who of you by worrying can add a single hour to his life?

And why do you worry about clothes? See how the lilies of the field grow. They do not labor or spin. Yet I tell you that not even Solomon in all his splendor was dressed like one of these. If that is how God clothes the grass of the field, which is here today and tomorrow is thrown into the fire, will he not much more clothe you, O you of little faith? So do not worry, saying, "What shall we eat?" or "What shall we drink?" or "What shall we wear?" For the pagans run after all these things, and your heavenly Father knows that you need them. But seek first his kingdom and his righteousness, and all these things will be given to you as well. Therefore do not worry about tomorrow, for tomorrow will worry about itself. Each day has enough trouble of its own.

Matthew 6:25-34

Jesus was more concerned with the internal attitude than external appearance anyway.

This brings us to a second key area: attitude. It is important to have a healthy view of sports. Sports are amoral — not good in themselves or bad either. But if played properly, a person has a tremendous opportunity to overcome the adversities inherent in competition, to demonstrate an attitude of tolerance and fair play, and best of all, to relate the love of Christ to others by participating. Also, since the body was made for motion, exercise is essential for its maximum function. Women need physical activity just as much as men.

Finally, it is vital to be a lady first and an athlete second in our actions. Be aware that it is easy to become a pushy, unsubmissive individual who always wants her own way. All athletes face this temptation, especially those who have experienced some success. But submission to others with humility is an attitude that honors God and one that God honors in return. Let His Word and the counsel of His Spirit guide your every action as you compete. Both your appearance and your character will blossom as you give Him first place in everything.

THINK IT OVER

What do the habits you develop have to do with your appearance in twenty years?

FOCUS ON THE FINISH LINE

Memorize 1 Timothy 4:8:

> *For physical training is of some value, but godliness has value for all things, holding promise for both the present life and the life to come.*

"DIFFERENT STROKES FOR DIFFERENT FOLKS"

Read Ephesians 5:22-33

IF A VOLLEYBALL TEAM is to be successful, each player must fulfill her appointed role. Players who play near the net must be good spikers and blockers, while others must serve and set up the shots. It is foolish and self-defeating for a spiker to step out of her role and try to set it up for a shorter player, or for a short "setter" to try to spike instead of setting it up for a taller one. On an efficient team, everyone fulfills her appointed role.

Just as there are basic roles to be played on any athletic team, there are different roles to be played by men and women for the good of both in society. While Scripture has little to say about a woman's role in government and in industry, it has much to say about her role in marriage and in the church. Contrary to the opinions of many today, God has created the sexes with basic differences and given them different responsibilities. Neither is inferior or superior. Each needs the other. Let's examine some of the many differences between the sexes and the implications for their functions in a man-woman relationship.

Neurologists have discovered that certain areas of the brain control specific behaviors. Women are generally more person-oriented, with earlier development of verbal and social skills than males (a left-brain function). Men have superior visual-spatial skills and can manipulate three-dimensional objects in their minds more easily (a right-brain function). Men are more acclimated to a world of things. Women are equipped to contribute a more personal touch to this impersonal world of things.

Physically, the average adult male is larger and stronger because of the male hormone (testosterone). The average female has a higher percentage of body fat (27% to 15%), a smaller bone and muscle mass, a smaller heart, less aerobic capacity (endurance), and a wider hip girth to facilitate child-birth. Differing joint structures make many young girls more flexible than boys. Emotionally, the female is affected by monthly changes in her body. Pre-menstrual syndrome (PMS) can cause one to quickly become emotional. Irritability, a quick temper, and poor sportsmanship often flare out of control during the menstrual cycle. Sexually, males tend to be aroused by sight (suggestive clothes, etc.) and females by touch — facts with obvious implications for hazards in dating relationships.

The point is this: today's idea of "unisex" is ungodly. Our Heavenly Father made the sexes distinct from one another, that each might compliment the other. Men should assume their God-given roles as providers and protectors, honoring women as the weaker partner.

> Husbands, in the same way be considerate as you live with your wives, and treat them with respect as the weaker partner and as heirs with you of the gracious gift of life, so that nothing will hinder your prayers.
>
> 1 Peter 3:7

Wives should find fulfillment in the role of helper and en-courager, submitting to their husbands.

> Wives, submit to your husbands as to the Lord.
>
> Ephesians 5:22

In so doing, both find that God's ideas on the subject are the best ideas.

THINK IT OVER

At your particular stage in life, how can you best fulfill your role as a godly woman in all your relationships?

FOCUS ON THE FINISH LINE

Memorize Philippians 2:13:

For it is God who works in you to will and to act according to His good purpose.

YOUR
BEST
POSITION

Read Romans 1:18-32

JUST AS A WISE VOLLEYBALL PLAYER knows her role on the team, a smart basketball player or coach knows where she best fits as well. It is foolish for a tall girl who can't dribble to play point guard. It would be equally unwise to post up a short girl against a tall opponent under the basket. Good coaches know the correct position for each athlete.

God knows that every girl is in the best position when she has healthy relationships with others. He made us and He gave us rules for our own good. All sexual activity between members of the same sex takes us out of our best position, causing us to worship self and others instead of God. Worshiping other people brings about severe consequences. Romans 1:26 says, "Because of this, God gave them over to shameful lusts. Even their women exchanged natural relations for unnatural ones." In other words, they left their natural positions to play "out of position."

Lesbianism can develop because a girl feels her father wants a boy and is unhappy with her as a girl. It may be encouraged by lack of meaningful relationships with boys. It may develop because of lack of emotional support, a painful past, or from pressure by an older woman. It may be fed by a desire for masculine traits which contribute to success in athletics. Feelings develop and the lesbian lifestyle delivers a drop of pleasure along with a gallon of depression, hurt, and alienation from God.

Feelings don't make one a lesbian. Yielding to wrong feelings is a conscious decision. The lesbian lifestyle is something folks walk into step by step. The problem is to *do* what is right when you feel like doing wrong. Everyone struggles with issues of right and wrong in different areas. Having a temptation is not evil, but it is hard!

The battleground is over one's will. An obese person may love hot-fudge sundaes. She may have loved them since she could remember. Can she just stop loving hot-fudge sundaes? Probably not. But she can seek God and yield to His help to *do* right. She can *decide* to eat differently. One with lesbian tendencies can *decide* not to act them out. She can change her circle of friends. It's a matter of the will to yield to God and seek His strength. He will help anyone who sincerely seeks Him.

THINK IT OVER
What is the best way for you to avoid sexual sin?

FOCUS ON THE FINISH LINE
Memorize Romans 1:25:
They exchanged the truth of God for a lie, and worshiped and served created things rather than the Creator — Who is forever praised. Amen.

BAD HABITS

How does Satan try to trip you up?

CONTROLLING
THE MOST POWERFUL
MUSCLE IN THE BODY

Read James 3

ZOLA BUDD OF SOUTH AFRICA was crushed by the results
of the women's 3000-meter run at the 1984 Los Angeles
Olympic Games. It wasn't that she was run into from behind
by Mary Decker, who fell down and caused both runners to
be unable to finish the race. The most devastating development was that Mary vehemently blamed Zola for the collision,
though clearly there was no fault to be found in Zola's running. The high regard which Zola Budd held for Mary Decker
was shattered by Mary's slander and accusations. Zola felt so
bad she even considered giving up a promising future in
international competition.

Whether we acknowledge it or not, our words have a
very powerful effect upon others. Concerning Napoleon and
his Italian campaign, Emil Leudwig said, "Half of what he
achieves is achieved by the power of words." By our words we
have the power to bless and encourage others, or to defeat
and destroy them. But more than the effect of our words
upon others, our words have a tremendous effect upon
ourselves. That's why slander and gossip are so destructive.
To paraphrase an old saying, "What Sue tells about Jane tells
more about Sue than it tells about Jane." We must keep our
words sweet, for we may have to eat them some day! In fact,
we ought not to even *listen* to gossip or slander that others
would share with us.

Because there are two sides to every story, we must be
very careful about criticizing others. We have not walked in
their shoes, and we may not know the whole story. When we
criticize others, we always hurt ourselves.

How do you handle the gossip and criticism which
someone has spread about you? First, analyze it. If there is
any validity in it, use it to help you improve. If it is unjust,
don't retaliate or try to defend yourself. Just forget it.

Do not answer a fool according to his folly, or you will be like him yourself.

Proverbs 26:4

Your friends don't need an explanation and your enemies won't believe you anyway. Jesus was the most criticized, but He never defended Himself. Turn the other cheek. Learn to love your enemies.

> You have heard it was said, "Love your neighbor and hate your enemy." But I tell you; Love your enemies and pray for those who persecute you. . . .
>
> Matthew 5:43-44

As John R. Bisagno says in *The Power of Positive Living*, "As you love them that hate you, you will find your enemies becoming your friends. While it may not change them at first, it will change you. They will like the new you, and you will like the new them. Your worst enemy may become your best friend."

THINK IT OVER

What is the key to controlling the "most powerful little muscle in your body?"

FOCUS ON THE FINISH LINE

Memorize Ephesians 4:29:

Do not let any unwholesome talk come out of your mouths, but only what is helpful for building others up according to their needs, that it may benefit those who listen.

THE ROCK
OF THIS WORLD
OR THE ROCK
OF THE AGES?

Read Romans 12:1-2

SUCCESS IN THE OLYMPIC GAMES is a fast way to greatly expand one's influence. Shortly after the 1996 Games, the entire women's gymnastics team was on a box of Wheaties. Women's soccer was elevated to a new high as our team defeated powerful China in the gold medal game before 76,000 fans. And Shannon Miller was added to the list of household names with a gold medal performance on the balance beam. Olympic success certainly gave all these female performers a powerful platform in America.

Music and movies provide another powerful platform through which to influence others. Many messages are being conveyed by the words and rhythm of the songs which program our thinking. Psychologists tell us that everything we've ever seen or heard is recorded subconsciously for future reference. Therefore, the music, movies, and television programs we see and hear are giving us a frame of reference from which we make decisions. If we are not on guard, we can go from the toleration of ideas which only seem to be a little "off base" to eventually embracing them as standards for living.

By their own admission, many rock composers and movie producers attempt to influence the actions of those who consume their products. Because of its widespread popularity, let's focus on the rock scene. Recent surveys show that over 85 percent of American teens listen to rock music an average of over two hours per day. That comes to a minimum of 5,000 hours (75,000 songs) for a person from age 13-19. What messages are being communicated? There are three main themes.

The first theme of the rock of this world is illicit sex. Elvis Costell said in *Time Magazine,* "Rock and roll is about sex . . . and I'm here to corrupt the youth of America." Other groups such as *Motley Crue* and *Quiet Riot* use graphic lyrics to portray cheap sex. David Lee Roth (*VanHalen*) says publicly, "I'm in the job to exercise my sexual fantasies. When I'm on stage it's like I'm doing it with 20,000 of your closest friends . . . I'm proud of the way we live." In *Circus Magazine* he said, "I've managed to live out 100 percent of my fantasies with pretty women I've met on the road. We celebrate all the sex and violence of television . . . that's *VanHalen*." *Pink Floyd* is explicit about their message with titles like "Young Lust," which has lyrics like, "I need a dirty woman." *Foreigner* sings lyrics in "Urgent" that portray cheap thrills of instant sex. They boast of not wanting a love that will last. Rod Steward (*Circus Magazine*) said, "A happy home life, security, and in-laws aren't conducive to making rock and roll." The perversion of *Led Zeppelin* and *KISS* are despicable, boasting of evil and sensuality. Elton John glorifies lesbianism in "All the Young Girls Love Alice." Several of these and other groups like the Pretenders promote sadomasochism (the beating and sexual abuse of a partner).

The second theme of the world's rock music is drug use. Glen Fry, formerly of the *Eagles,* says, "I'm in the music business for the sex and narcotics." After becoming a mother, Grace Slick of *Jefferson Starship* said, "It's hard to keep an eye on the kid while you're hallucinating." The list of rock stars who have died of drug overdoses is staggering. *Starship's* Paul Kanter, the lead guitarist who has been busted on numerous occasions, bragged that he had so much cocaine it "got to the point where you couldn't breathe." When asked about the cost, he replied, "The group paid for it; it was a business expense."

The third theme of this world's rock is worship of Satan. Styx uses Satanic symbols on their clothing and album covers. In fact, the word Styx is the name of a river surrounding hell in ancient mythology. *AC/DC,* in "Highway to Hell," tries to make hell sound attractive and tries to make kids lure their friends to go there. Numerous other groups like *Meat Loaf* have promoted worship of the Evil One.

Rebellion against authority and promotion of eastern religions are also motives of many rock musicians. Certainly, the world's rock music does not promote godliness. Nor does some country music, with its themes of unfaithfulness, divorce, and alcoholism. Nor does the melancholy of blues music. Nor do movies and TV shows which treat drinking alcohol and sexual sins as socially acceptable.

A follower of Christ must be alert for *all* evil influences.

It is not possible for a Christian to have a vital, healthy walk with Jesus and to bombard his or her mind with messages contrary to His Word and will. As Author Tim LaHaye points out in "How to Win Over Depression," "Modern music is not necessarily Satanic, but the natural result of eliminating Jesus Christ from one's life. Unless filled with the Holy Spirit, the musician creates morbid, pessimistic, negative music with a detrimental beat. This leads to an unhealthy emotional development." Other psychologists cite the addictive and unnatural beat of rock and the escapism it provides.

What kind of life do you desire? Do you really want to walk with God? Then you'll have to be still before Him.

> Be still and know that I am God; I will be exalted among the nations, I will be exalted in the earth.
>
> Psalm 46:10

You will have to listen to His voice.

> A voice came from the cloud, saying, "This is my Son, whom I have chosen; listen to him."
>
> Luke 9:35

You cannot hold to the world's values and be a close follower of Jesus. Your moods, your mind set, and your values must be from God, not from this world system. You are to be transformed.

> With eyes wide open to the mercies of God, I beg you, my brothers, as an act of intelligent worship, to give him your bodies, as a living sacrifice, consecrated to him and acceptable by him. Don't let the world around you squeeze you into its own mold, but let God re-make you so that your whole attitude of mind is changed. . . .
>
> Romans 12:1-2 (J. B. Phillips)

Be very careful what thoughts fill your mind. The rock of this evil world will not draw you to the Rock of *ALL* Ages!

THINK IT OVER

What value system is dictating your decisions?

FOCUS ON THE FINISH LINE

Memorize Romans 12:2 (Phillips):

Don't let the world around you squeeze you into its own mold, but let God re-make you so that your whole attitude of mind is changed.

ONE WAY
2 PLAY

Read Ephesians 5:15-18

PRO GOLFER BETSY KING has much to say about alcohol and drugs. "I have always avoided drugs and alcohol because I knew they could only hurt my athletic performance. Even before I was a Christian, I had strong feelings about drinking and drugs. I didn't want anything to prevent me from doing my best on the course.

"One of the big factors in whether you drink is who you hang around. If you hang around a wild group of people, then drinking and drugs will be more of a temptation. I made some choices all along the way to spend time with people who cared about the things I cared about. Wild parties just weren't attractive to me. Following Christ and athletic performance were — and are — important to me."

Alcohol, nicotine, and other drugs hurt you as an athlete. But more importantly, drugs will hurt you personally in every area of life. They cause girls to do things they would not do otherwise. You never know when addiction will occur. Girls are more susceptible to the effects of alcohol because they have less of a digestive enzyme than guys have (that doesn't make drinking right for guys, either). Your body adapts to whatever you put into it, and some people are addicted after one drink! You'll never realize your potential as a person if you use drugs.

Girls use drugs for several reasons: to appear grown up, to assert independence, to be accepted by peers who smoke or drink, to escape emotional pain, as an experiment, to express anger, or because parents use drugs in some form. But any substance that takes control of you is sin. We are to be controlled by God's Holy Spirit. Ephesians 5:18 says, "Be filled with the Spirit." We are to continually be under His control, for our bodies belong to God.

Do you not know that your body is a temple of the Holy

Spirit, who is in you, whom you have received from God? You are not your own; you were bought at a price. Therefore honor God with your body.

1 Corinthians 6:19-20

Furthermore, we must not cause others to stumble into the use of alcohol, nicotine, or other drugs by doing so ourselves.

It is better not to eat meat or drink wine or to do anything else that will cause your brother to fall.

Romans 14:21

We will all "reap what we sow" (Galatians 6:7). But we always reap more than we sow and we reap it later. Drug use is progressive. Beer and wine coolers often lead to hard liquor, cigarettes lead to marijuana, and cocaine often leads to crack or heroin. The amount of drug that brings a high today must be increased to produce the same high tomorrow. This is the scary truth.

Here's another scary truth: Addictions begin as a sinful choice, but once the body physiologically adapts to the chemical, a person has a terrible disease. She becomes chemically dependent instead of dependent upon a loving heavenly Father.

So, don't use drugs. If you have drunk alcohol, smoked tobacco or tried other drugs and can't give them up, get help from a counselor — and from the Lord Jesus. There really is only "one way 2 play" — and it's drug-free.

THINK IT OVER

What do you want to become in life? What effect would drugs have upon your goals?

FOCUS ON THE FINISH LINE

Memorize Romans 13:14:

Let us behave decently, as in the daytime, not in orgies and drunkenness, not in sexual immorality and debauchery, not in dissension and jealousy. Rather, clothe yourselves with the Lord Jesus Christ, and do not think about how to gratify the desires of the sinful nature.

TO EAT
OR NOT
TO EAT . . .

Read Ephesians 2:1-10

AT THE PEAK of her world-class gymnastics career,
Christy Henrich was 4'10" and weighed 95 pounds. But when
she died on July 26, 1994, she was 22 years old and weighed
61 pounds. At one point she had weighed only 47 pounds.
Christy died of multiple organ failure caused by malnutrition.
Her eating disorder was driven by an abnormal desire to lose
weight to excel in gymnastics. At one point she told the
Independence (Missouri) *Examiner,* "My life is a horrifying
nightmare. It feels like there's a beast inside me, like a
monster. It feels evil."

Eating disorders are the most serious health problem
facing female athletes. Statistics show at least 62 percent of
girls competing in figure skating, gymnastics, and endurance
sports suffer from eating disorders. Girls who are perfectionists, depressed, have low self-esteem, or are victims of sexual
abuse are most susceptible.

A civil war goes on in the minds of many girls. They
feel dirty, unworthy, degraded, and obese. They feel unworthy to eat, so they starve themselves. They are usually
perfectionists, wanting to see everything fixed in their lives.
But no one can fix everything in a fallen, evil world, so not
measuring up to perfection, they starve themselves. The
condition is called anorexia and it affects mostly the high-
economic achievers who have insecure, rigid, self-critical
feelings. They refuse to eat and engage in compulsive exercise to the point where their body starts to digest its own lean
muscle tissue. Often they hear voices of condemnation in
their minds.

A newer and related emotional problem is called
bulimia or "ox-hunger." In this abnormality, girls alternately
diet, eat like an ox, then induce vomiting to rid themselves of
calories. Bulimics often skip meals, give food away and
exercise compulsively. They are often outgoing people who

have extreme emotional ups and downs. The problem affects two million American women. The constant inner tension, low self-esteem, guilt, depression, and need to compare with others drives the viscous cycle. Even Christian girls can be affected.

The unconditional love of Jesus Christ and His servants is the answer to the emotional needs of girls with eating disorders. Often they have lost the will to live. Jesus loves you and died for you. He knows you are valuable enough to die for. Once you accept His love and see yourself as He sees you, you regain the God-given instinct to live. He enables you to live abundantly! You are His workmanship! As you believe the truth and act upon it your feelings return. There is great hope in Jesus!

THINK IT OVER

Do you have a tendency towards eating disorders? Will you seek help from God and a Christian friend?

FOCUS ON THE FINISH LINE
Memorize Ephesians 2:10:

For we are God's workmanship, created in Christ Jesus to do good works, which God prepared in advance for us to do.

Tough Times

How do you handle problems?

SOMETIMES I FEEL LIKE "THE LONE RANGERETTE"

Hurdle #25

Read Isaiah 53

ATHLETICS, LIKE EVERY OTHER PART OF LIFE, present us with both pain and pleasure, toil and comfort, and high and low points in competition. In Berlin's 1936 Olympic Games, Rie Mastenbroek of Holland fought from behind to gain a one-meter victory in the 400-meter freestyle. In fact, she won a total of three gold medals and one silver medal as a swimmer in those games. But Rie had a most difficult life after the Olympics. She was divorced and worked fourteen hours a day as a cleaning woman to support her children. She told *Sports Illustrated* in 1972, "I am forgotten. No one remembers who I was . . . Sometimes I think, 'Oh, dear, oh, dear, how good I must have been, how really good!'" The crowd which had once applauded her now turned away, leaving her in her loneliness.

God never promised the Christian that she'd never have some lonely feelings in this life. But He did promise "Never will I leave you; never will I forsake you" (Hebrews 13:5). Therefore, the promises of God are the cure for loneliness! In spite of the fact that we may be going through a valley, we are never really left alone. One who is living for Christ may be left out if she is the only Christian on the team. To talk to some people about the Lord Jesus is to risk their rejection. But we must obey God and present the claims of Christ anyway. Refusing to drink alcohol at a party, or to experiment just once with drugs, or to participate in lesbianism or other sexual sin may leave us outside the group's "inner circle." But we must refuse anyway, for the end result of these sins is devastation. We are to have nothing to do with these "fruitless deeds of darkness" (Ephesians 5:11). A life of addiction, mental depression, suicidal tendencies, and shattered marriages awaits those who think they can live for today and postpone the consequences. It is much better to say "no" to "worldly passions" (Titus 2:12) and experience the world's rejection than to indulge and suffer more painful results. God's severe discipline awaits those who succumb in these areas.

While going against the crowd is not popular, it does earn the respect of others. It will earn an admiration for traits that lost people wish they had, but which they are too weak to receive. Remember that Jesus was "despised and rejected" (Isaiah 53:3). Accept the same for His sake when you must take a stand. Thank God for the opportunity to glorify Him before your peers. You'll be glad you did!

> And anyone who does not carry his cross and follow me cannot be my disciple.
>
> Luke 14:27

THINK IT OVER

What will be your response when you experience rejection because of your commitment to Christ?

FOCUS ON THE FINISH LINE
Memorize Matthew 5:11:

Blessed are you when people insult you, persecute you and falsely say all kinds of evil against you because of Me.

"MY TEAMMATE DROPPED THE BALL AND COACH YELLED AT ME!"

Hurdle #26

Read 1 Peter 2

MARGARET MURDOCK knows what its like to battle against odds that don't seem fair. Overcoming a severe visual impairment, she competed in the 1976 Olympic Games in riflery, an event that was dominated by men. Despite the responsibility of a young child throughout her practice schedule, Margaret went on to become the first woman to win a silver medal in the event!

Let's face it — life is not always fair. Innocent people suffer. Sometimes we are rewarded when we shouldn't be rewarded and at other times we are unjustly punished. We get yelled at when someone else drops the ball! We experience social, racial, and even religious prejudice. How can we survive in such a crazy, mixed-up world? Maybe these pointers can help:

1. Remember that suffering is not brought on us by God because He hates us. Suffering is a result of man's sin in turning away from God. Because of the fall of Adam and Eve, sin and suffering came into the world. God is good and He hurts when we suffer.

2. Remember that God is Sovereign. He does allow us to experience some suffering. But, for the Christian, He has a purpose in it. He desires that we "be conformed to the image of Jesus" (Romans 8:29) through every trial we experience.

3. We can therefore be thankful in suffering, even when it is unjust! If we are yelled at for something we did wrong, we can change our ways. If we have suffered unfairly, we remember that Jesus was treated unfairly on the cross. He didn't deserve

what He got. We don't deserve His righteousness, but because of His unjust suffering for us, we receive His imputed righteousness when we trust Him as Savior. That's not fair, but aren't we glad? Freedom comes when we remember His suffering and surrender all our "rights" to Him, thanking Him in all circumstances. Then we become truly grateful that we don't get what we really deserve!

Next time you suffer, remember the Lord Jesus Christ and be thankful. You have a Savior who knows the real meaning of injustice and who can help you rise above it!

THINK IT OVER

When you are treated unfairly, how can you handle the circumstance in a way that pleases God?

FOCUS ON THE FINISH LINE

Memorize 1 Peter 2:21:

To this you were called, because Christ suffered for you, leaving you an example, that you should follow in his steps.

WHEN YOU FEEL LIKE CHECKING IN FOR KEEPS

Hurdle #27

Read Psalm 18

JUNE 4, 1986, WILL FOREVER BE ETCHED into the memory of North Carolina State's Kathy Ormsby. It was a day when the pressures of life seemingly overwhelmed the NCAA's 10,000-meter record holder. While competing in the 10,000-meter race at the NCAA Outdoor Championships in Indianapolis, the dean's list student in pre-med suddenly left the track, ran out of the stadium, scaled a 7-foot chain link fence, and jumped off a bridge over the White River. She was critically injured and paralyzed from the waist down. Kathy shared these feelings:

> "All of a sudden . . . I just felt like something snapped inside of me," she said. "And I was really angry. I felt like it was so unfair. All of a sudden I didn't feel like this was me because I didn't usually have reactions like that. I do think God wants us to do our best, but I don't think He wants us to be obsessed with that or to do it in such a way that it doesn't leave time for ourselves to enjoy life."

Suicide is the third leading cause of death among young people, annually claiming 5,000 youth between the ages of fifteen and twenty-four. Mental health experts estimate that up to 5,500 young people attempt suicide each day! It is a serious temptation, obviously faced by many kids in our culture. The loss of moral absolutes in America has led to feelings of hopelessness which contribute to the urge to self-destruct. Though no one is immune from suicidal thoughts, they can and must be overcome and dismissed.

Why is it imperative for the Christian to overcome this temptation? After all, if God has saved our soul, why can't we just "check into heaven" a little early? There are several reasons why suicide is not a valid option. First, we have the supernatural power of the living God to overcome the world.

> For God did not give us a spirit of timidity, but a spirit of power, of love, and of self-discipline.
>
> 2 Timothy 1:7

Second, the real purpose of our life is to glorify our God, and He is glorified when we overcome the evil one. But when a person destroys himself, Satan is given ammunition to discredit the Lord and His power. We must not give the devil such opportunity for slander of our Father! God's overcoming power works when we exercise it! Suicide is like abortion — a terrible waste of the potential God has for a life. God wants to do so much for us and in us while we live — but once we die, we have lost opportunities to grow, to earn rewards in heaven, and to triumph on earth in the midst of trials. Far better to "hang in there" and see what an omnipotent God will do, even in impossible situations!

Pray about everything. Ask God to intervene with His power to help you focus on the positives. Let a godly Christian help and encourage you through the rough spots. Stay physically active *doing* what you know God has given you to do. Show your trust in God and His Word by reading and studying it for the answers to problems. The Psalms are especially helpful to redirect one's thoughts towards God and off of ourselves. There is hope — and it is found only in Him!

THINK IT OVER

If Christ has saved you, meditate upon the promise God has made to you to help you in this life. As you trust in Him, bring honor and not disgrace to Him by your actions.

FOCUS ON THE FINISH LINE

Memorize Psalm 55:22:

Cast your cares on the Lord and He will sustain you; He will never let the righteous fall.

THE ANTIDOTE FOR STRESS

Hurdle #28

Read Psalm 46

SARAH DEVENS WAS A RARE ATHLETE. She played three varsity sports at Dartmouth — field hockey, ice hockey, and lacrosse — and captained all three! One season merged with the next and she never slowed down. All three teams needed her. She made the U.S. field hockey "B" team. Exhausted and caught in a crossfire of expectations, the 21-year-old senior-to-be took her own life in the summer of 1995.

The stress of life takes a severe toll on the lives of people today. As if the daily stress we face isn't enough, we find things change so fast we are stressed out just trying to keep up! Toeffler (1971) referred to this as a state of "future shock."

Hans Selye defines stress as the "nonspecific response of the body to a demand." In other words, the body makes responses to the pressures of life. These responses vary with each individual. They can include an increased heart rate, increased blood pressure, release of stress hormones, an upset stomach, tension headaches, and a stiff neck in the short run and heart disease, ulcers, skin problems, and even cancer in the long run. Our bodies produce adrenaline for emergencies, but we are living such "revved up" lives we are living daily on this "high octane" fuel! Something has to give!

Dr. Bettie Young calls stress "a twentieth-century disease affecting young and old." With our complex comput-ers, multiple options brought about by the internet, speed of travel across the country, cellular phones and fax machines, we have greatly accelerated the pace of life. We become used to 15-second commercials which pump us up, spin us around, and spit us out! Rock music, the monotonous tone of television, diets loaded with sugar and fats which greatly alter body chemistry, pressure to please significant others, family breakups, worries about school, and monthly menstrual cycles all contribute to our stress level. The list goes on and on! Some researchers say that 15 percent of kids are highly susceptible to stress from the moment of birth because of their mother's mental attitude and diet!

How do you handle stress? The best antidote for stress is trust in an Almighty God who loves and cares for you as a person. We don't need to worry when we can trust Him! Worry is like racing a car's engine when the transmission is in neutral! God is still on the throne and He still can act! Stop, identify your sources of stress, and calmly give them to Him. Spending time alone with God in a quiet place, physical exercise, soothing music, and sharing with a close friend helps so much. "A cheerful heart is good medicine, but a crushed spirit dries up the bones" (Proverbs 17:22). We really do need Him and each other!

There is no substitute for praising and thanking God. Find a church where praise to God lifts the spirits of everyone who worships there. God loves it when we praise Him, and when we do, He comes even closer to us.

THINK IT OVER

How do you handle stress? What could you do to handle it more effectively?

FOCUS ON THE FINISH LINE

Memorize Psalm 46:10:

Be still and know that I am God.

RECOVERY

What if you've fallen?

WHEN THE PAST HINDERS YOUR FUTURE

Hurdle #29

Read Philippians 3:1-14

IN RACQUETBALL, AN OPPONENT cannot block one's view of the front wall or impede the ball on its way to the wall. When that happens, a "hinder" is called and the point is replayed. It's a simple rule that keeps players focused on the object of the game instead of the opponent.

Many women are "hindered" by regret of past deeds they have done or failed to do. Everyone has painful memories of past sins, failures, mistakes, and opportunities that were missed. We wonder what life would be like if only . . . . But when we focus too much on wrong turns in the road of life, regret imprisons us behind bars of guilt, depression, self-pity, or indecision. Regret poisons our future, as emotions overwhelm common sense. Katherine Mansfield writes, "Regret is an appalling waste of energy: You can't build on it. It's only good for wallowing in." The past must be called for a "hinder" in the game of life. How can it be done?

Refuse to dwell on the past. Do you think you are perfect? No one has lived mistake-free. No one is on God's "Plan A." He has a great way of taking our mistakes and turning them into something positive. Think on the good things you have done and how they have benefited others.

> Whatever is true, whatever is noble, whatever is right, whatever is pure, whatever is lovely, whatever is admirable — if anything is excellent or praiseworthy — think about such things.
>
> Philippians 4:8

You must exercise your will to think only on these things.

Focus on the future. In a round of golf, if you make a bad shot, you can still have a great round if you look ahead and don't dwell on the bad one. Never let regrets replace dreams!

Do something for someone else. Since regret is self-centered, turning your attention to someone else takes your mind off self and regret has no chance to hinder you anymore!

Forgive yourself as God has forgiven you. We are commanded to forgive others, but often find it even harder to forgive ourselves. If we've confessed our sin to God, He has buried our sins in the deepest sea and posted a "no fishing" sign. Thank Him for His forgiveness. Praise Him continually.

Dreams about tomorrow can stop regret every time it creeps back into the back of your mind. The best is yet to come. Keep looking to Jesus and the future and Satan and the past will be bound and gagged in your life!

THINK IT OVER
What is the best strategy to triumph over your past?

FOCUS ON THE FINISH LINE
Memorize Philippians 2:13-14:

But one thing I do: Forgetting what is behind and straining toward what is ahead, I press on toward the goal to win the prize for which God has called me heavenward in Christ Jesus.

WOUNDED
ON THE INSIDE

Read 1 John 1

HELENE MADISON was a 1932 Olympic champion swimmer. "She could out swim any woman on earth," wrote Royal Brougham of the *Seattle Post-Intelligencer*. But she dropped from sight after winning 23 national championships and breaking every world record.

Thirty years later Brougham found Helene sitting in a one-room basement apartment in despondency. Desperately ill and forgotten by the world, the former champion was planning to drive her car to a dead-end road, close the windows, and kill herself via carbon monoxide poisoning. Her body was full of cancer. Brougham convinced her to change her mind and seek help.

A year later Helene died, but full of hope. Brougham wrote, "At long last, Helene Madison placed her thin, frail hand into the hand of a bedside counselor and asked the Lord Jesus to come into her heart. She found the peace she had unsuccessfully sought in so many byways."

Many women have tripped over the hurdle of moral purity and fallen badly. The wounds go much deeper than a skinned knee or a bruise. But, because of the love and healing power of a wonderful Heavenly Father, there is great hope — the same hope Helene Madison found.

Here are some practical tips for dealing with past sin of having had sex outside of marriage. Find an older, godly female who loves Jesus and confess your sin to her. As we confess our sins to each other and pray for one another we can expect healing.

> Therefore confess your sins to each other and pray for each other so that you may be healed. The prayer of a righteous man is powerful and effective.
>
> James 5:15

God has promised to forgive us when we confess our sins, so you must forgive yourself.

> If we confess our sins, he is faithful and just and will forgive us our sins and purify us from all unrighteousness.
>
> 1 John 1:9

Determine by the grace of God to live a pure and holy life. Meditate upon the Word of God and avoid situations where Satan might again tempt you by carefully choosing your companions.

> Blessed is the man who does not walk in the counsel of the wicked or stand in the way of sinners or sit in the seat of mockers. But his delight is in the law of the LORD, and on his law he meditates day and night. He is like a tree planted by streams of water, which yields its fruit in season and whose leaf does not wither. Whatever he does prospers. Not so the wicked! They are like chaff that the wind blows away. Therefore the wicked will not stand in the judgment, nor sinners in the assembly of the righteous. For the LORD watches over the way of the righteous, but the way of the wicked will perish.
>
> Psalm 1

When Satan accuses you (and he will) of past forgiven sin, remind him that the blood of Jesus purifies us of every sin.

> But if we walk in the light, as he is in the light, we have fellowship with one another, and the blood of Jesus, his Son, purifies us from all sin.
>
> 1 John 1:7

Many others have tried to "fix" a teen pregnancy problem via abortion. If that is your situation, God still loves and forgives! The devil has lied to you concerning the seriousness of abortion. You will go through several stages before inner healing comes. After an immediate sense of relief, you will rationalize the killing of your baby by saying, "I had to do it," or "It was just a blob of tissue." Then the realization and shock of what you did will set in, along with a sense of bewilderment. Denial may return or you may proceed to the most painful part of the grieving process: anger, depression, and regret. You must seek God and the counsel of a strong believer. Seek the forgiveness of God and accept it. Christ died for all sin, including this one. Forgive others who betrayed you during the pregnancy and the abortion. Surrender your anger, bitterness and self-hatred to Christ daily. They will destroy you if you don't. As you walk with Him, realize that you can only go on by His grace. But you can go on! Your self-esteem will return when you get beyond yourself and focus on the Lord and on helping others.

God heals the brokenhearted and binds up their inner wounds.

> He heals the brokenhearted and binds up their wounds.
>
> Psalm 147:3

He works through much prayer, the godly counsel of other Christians, a mind set on His Word, and His Holy Spirit. There is great hope for those who seek His face.

THINK IT OVER

Have you sought God's inner healing for the deep hurts of your life? He wants to heal your heart even more than you want to be free from the guilt of sin.

FOCUS ON THE FINISH LINE

Memorize 1 John 1:9:

If we confess our sins, he is faithful and just and will forgive us our sins, and purify us from all unrighteousness.

PICKING UP
THE PIECES

Read Psalm 51

TWENTY-ONE-YEAR-OLD THIRD BASEMAN DANI TYLER did
something she would like to forget during an 1996 Olympic
softball game against Australia. She hit what would have been
a game-winning home-run in the fifth inning of a scoreless tie,
but missed home plate in her rush to high-five a teammate.
Australia appealed, the umpire called her out, and the USA
team lost 2-1 in extra innings. "I'm the one who lost the
game," she said.

Some girls have made much bigger mistakes than
missing home plate and costing the team an Olympic softball
game. One such mistake is to have an abortion. Abortion is
not only murder of an innocent baby, but it traumatizes the
mother. Post-Abortion Syndrome is very real. It involves the
chronic inability to process thoughts and emotions, to grieve,
and to find peace with God and others. Our society denies the
emotional pain which girls feel unable to discuss. Therefore,
the personal and moral dilemma is often unresolved.

A girl who has had an abortion may become numb to
the external world, feel guilty that she survived when her baby
didn't, have sleep disturbances, impaired memory or concen-
tration, and feel isolated. She may mentally relive the trauma
of the abortion and be repelled by medical personnel and even
vacuum cleaners. Seeing children the age her aborted child
would have been may bring further grief. Some women don't
allow themselves to feel and avoid intimate relationships.

Denial is the most common reaction to the trauma of
abortion. But a loss has taken place and the girl must be
allowed to grieve before healing can occur. A pregnancy was
and always will have taken place. No one ever told the girl it
would hurt so bad. Only God can heal such deep hurt. But He
often uses Christian ladies who can help "pick up the pieces"

of a broken heart. God can and will heal the heart of one who genuinely seeks Him.

THINK IT OVER

Who can you go to confess sin and receive healing on the inside?

FOCUS ON THE FINISH LINE

Memorize Psalm 51:1:

Have mercy on me, O God, according to your unfailing love; according to your great compassion blot out my transgressions.

RUNNING
TO WIN

Read Hebrews 12

GREEK MYTHOLOGY tells the story of Atalanta, a huntress who was nursed from infancy by a bear. She was a great hunter and could outrun any man. Upon reaching marriageable age, she turned down every man who desired her. "I will only marry the man who can outrun me," she said.

Atalanta proceeded to defeat and humiliate all challengers and her father had all the suitors killed! Along came Hippomenes (named Milanion in some books). He knew he could not outrun Atalanta, so he thought hard of another way to beat her and claim her hand in marriage. After a long time in thought, Hippomenes came up with a plan.

The race began and with a great burst of speed he knew he could not maintain, Hippomenes took the lead. As Atalanta got close, he pulled a golden apple out of a bag, dropped it, and kept running. Knowing she could pass him easily, Atalanta sopped to pick up the golden object. Moments later she was ready to pass him again, and Hippomenes dropped another golden apple. She picked it up. The farther they ran, the heavier Atalanta's load became. By the time he had rid himself of his load and she had picked up every apple, he easily won the race, and the hand of Atalanta.

Hebrews 12:1 tells us to "throw off everything that hinders and the sin that so easily entangles" in the race of life. Hippomenes rid himself of weight as Atalanta weighed herself down. As a result, he won the race. If you want to run life's races to win, you must strip off all sinful habits and attitudes. Your Master Coach, Jesus Christ, will help you as you go to Him in prayer and ask Him to take your heavy burdens from you so you can run to win. He never fails to lead His people to victory!

THINK IT OVER

Have you handed your heavy weights to the Lord Jesus? If not, why not?

FOCUS ON THE FINISH LINE

Memorize Hebrews 12:1:

Therefore, since we are surrounded by such a great cloud of witnesses, let us throw off everything that hinders and the sin that so easily entangles, and let us run with perseverance the race marked out for us.

Appendix

Appendix I
The Winning Run

PERHAPS YOU HAVE READ this book, but never personally trusted the Savior with your earthly life and your eternal destiny. The following softball illustration explains how you can come to know the Lord Jesus Christ:

In softball, a runner must touch all four bases to score a run for his team. The path to abundant and eternal life is very similar to the base paths on a ball diamond.

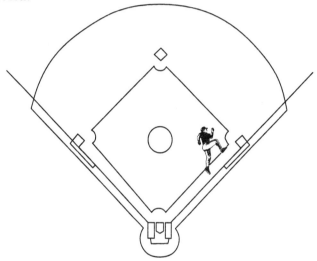

Step 1 (FIRST BASE) along that path is realizing that God cares about you. He not only created you, but He also loves you very deeply. He is seeking to give you an abundant life now and for eternity.

For God so loved the world that He gave His one and only Son, that whoever believes in Him shall not perish but have eternal life.

John 3:16

I have come that they may have life, and have it to the fullest.

John 10:10

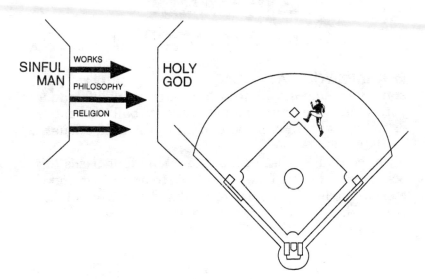

At SECOND BASE (step 2) we admit that we are sinners and separated from God. He is perfect, pure, and good; we are not. Because by nature we disobey Him and resist Him, He cannot have fellowship with us without denying His goodness and holiness. Instead, He must judge us.

Whoever believes in Him is not condemned; but whoever does not believe stands condemned already, because he has not believed in the name of God's one and only Son.
John 3:18

We realize we can never reach God through our own efforts. They do not solve the problem of our sin.

For all have sinned and come short of the glory of God.
Romans 3:23

But your iniquities have separated you from your God; your sins have hidden His face from you, so that He will not hear.

Isaiah 59:2

For the wages of sin is death, but the gift of God is eternal life in Christ Jesus our Lord.

Romans 6:23

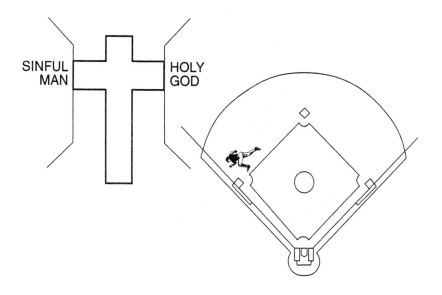

THIRD BASE is so close to scoring. Here (step 3) we understand that God has sent His Son, Jesus Christ, to die on the cross in payment for our sins. By His sacrifice, we may advance Home.

But God demonstrates His own love for us in this: While we were still sinners, Christ died for us.

Romans 5:8

For Christ died for sins once for all, the righteous for the unrighteous, to bring you to God.

I Peter 3:18

Jesus answered, "I am the way and the truth and the life. No one comes to the Father except through Me."

John 14:6

However, being CLOSE to Home does NOT count!

The Winning Run!

To score (step 4), we must personally receive Jesus Christ as Savior and Lord of our lives. We must not only realize that He died to rescue people from their sin but we must also trust Him to rescue us from our own sin. We cannot "squeeze" ourselves home any other way, and He will not force Himself upon us.

Yet to all who received Him, to those who believed in His name, He gave the right to become children of God.

John 1:12

For it is by grace you have been saved, through faith — and this is not from yourselves, it is the gift of God — not by works, so that no one can boast.

Ephesians 2:8-9

Why not receive Jesus Christ as your Savior and Lord right now? Simply say: "Yes, Lord," to His offer to forgive you for your sins and to change you.

_____

(signed)

_____

(date)

Tell someone of your decision and keep studying God's Word. These things greatly strengthen you (Romans 10:9-10). You may write *Cross Training Publishing* for further encouragement. We would be thrilled to hear of your commitment! Welcome to eternal life!

CROSS TRAINING PUBLISHING
P.O. BOX 1541
GRAND ISLAND, NE 68802

Appendix II

A Ballplayer's Paraphrase of 1 Corinthians 13:1-8

If I excel in the contest and speak loudly about it, but have not love, I am merely making noise.

If I know the game and have faith in my abilities, but have no love for teammates, coaches, fans, and opponents, I am nothing.

If I give autographs, money, or attention to others but have no love, it counts for nothing.

Love is patient; it shags balls for others while they're hitting. Love is kind; it allows the other person to step ahead into the batting cage. Love is not jealous of a teammate's perfect day. Love does not boast about the times I've gone 4 for 4. It is not arrogant about a championship.

Love does not act unbecomingly with cutting remarks about a teammate or opponent. Love seeks not its own interests but those of others first. It is not provoked by the heckling of opponents or fans; keeps no list of bad decisions by scorekeepers.

Love rejoices not in a home town call but rejoices in the integrity and honesty of umpires.

Love bears up in everything, is not unduly suspicious of others, never stops hoping, and persists doggedly until the end in all circumstances.

There are great achievements in softball, spectacular plays on the field, and superior strategy in the dugout. These all fade, but love remains — it never strikes out.